# A Catalogue Of Drawings Illustrating The Life Of General Washington, And Of Colonial Life

## Howard Pyle

In the interest of creating a more extensive selection of rare historical book reprints, we have chosen to reproduce this title even though it may possibly have occasional imperfections such as missing and blurred pages, missing text, poor pictures, markings, dark backgrounds and other reproduction issues beyond our control. Because this work is culturally important, we have made it available as a part of our commitment to protecting, preserving and promoting the world's literature. Thank you for your understanding.

# A Catalogue of Drawings

Illuftrating the Life of

## GEN. WASHINGTON,

AND OF

## COLONIAL LIFE.

Together with a few other Examples of work done for the Public Prints, by Howard Pyle.

---

Exhibited originally at the Drexel Inftitute of Art, Science and Induftry, in Philadelphia, now again put upon exhibition at the St. Botolph Club of Bofton, upon the Twenty-feventh of February next.

---

WILMINGTON:

Printed for the St. Botolph Club, by John M. Rogers, on Orange Street oppofite the Old Malt Houfe.

1897.

FA 6300.1-

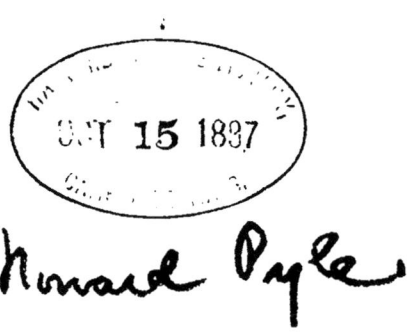

Howard Pyle

Copyright 1897, by John M. Rogers,
Wilmington, Del.

# A CATALOGUE OF Illuftrations

By Howard Pyle.

---

Exhibited by the St. BOTOLPH Club
for the Entertainment of its Friends,
at No. 2 Newbury Street, in Bofton.

## PREFACE.
### To a Second Edition.

IT sometimes happens that an author finds himself vastly surprised at the manner in which some modest effort to entertain has been received by his Readers. Such, in a measure, hath been the emotion of the Writer of this descriptive effusion. For he professes that he did not in the least suspect that a critical Publick would care to bestow any serious Consideration upon so slight a Production; still less did he suppose that a demand would be made upon him for a Second Edition thereof.

For it can hardly be necessary to call the Attention of the discerning Reader to the Fact that the Imprint—of which a new Edition is herewith offered for his Consideration—was prepared in such a lighter Mood as a Writer may bestow upon a Subject when he seizes his Pen to entertain a few appreciative Friends with his lucubrations. Therefore it is that, seeing so considerable an Attention directed upon his work as to demand a Renewal of his Effort, the Writer finds himself

self laboring under a Conflict of Emotion not diffimilar to that which may poffefs a modeft Man, who, embarking upon a mild Pleafantry which he directs to his neareft Neighbor, finds of a fudden the whole Table fallen filent to liften to him.

Whether or no a complacent Publick amufes itfelf with the Fancy that it hath difcovered in the Paragraphs herein fet before it, a flavor, however flight, of the Style in which the late Dr. Franklin may have written, certain it is that the Writer cannot difabufe himfelf of the Feeling that he hath gained the Attention of his Readers, not fo much by reafon of his own Merits, as becaufe of a certain Style which he hath borrowed and in which he hath enveloped himfelf, as did the Creature in the Fable. Whereupon he finds himfelf befet by an Apprehenfion left, in a Repetition of his Performance, his Difguife may be difcovered, and that Illufion which poffeffed his Readers difpelled.

However, he may plead in his own behalf that a re-iffue of his Work is neceffary, infomuch that the prefent Occafion demands fomething of the Sort. For that which the Author may claim as a Firft Edition of the following Catalogue, was defigned for an Exhibition of his Work under the Aufpices of the Drexel Inftitute of Philadelphia, whence the Pictures under prefent Confideration were tranfported bodily to a new Lodging Place, under the friendly Care of the St. Botolph Club of Bofton.

Accordingly it is for the Benefit of the Author's Patrons who fhall view his Efforts, as they hang in that
Elegant

Elegant and Genteel Resort, that he now ventures to reprint this descriptive Comment upon the works presented, altering here and there such passages as may fit it to the present Circumstances and Surroundings, and spicing it with such an Explanation as he fancies may suit it to other Tastes than those for whom it was originally designed.

In Conclusion he hath only to say that he entertains the Hope that that which was intended to amuse may not, by its Repetition, (like the Joke of a would-be Wit) tire them whom it was designed to entertain.

Such are the varied Reasons which the Author ventures to offer to his Patrons in this Apology for a Second Edition of so slight a Thing. Wherefore having eased his Mind so far as it may be discharged of its Doubts, he now proceeds to call the Attention of the indulgent Reader to the general prefatory Remarks and to the detailed Description that follows.

Wilmington, Feb. 24th, 1897.

Preface

# PREFACE.

THERE are, I suppose, not above twelve Artists out of an hundred who can present a set of their own Pictures to a Publick Audience with a perfectly sober Countenance and an easy Assurance as to the Merit of their Productions. This, I am well aware, is altogether contrary to the universal Opinion which accredits Fellows of that Craft with being of a free and easy Disposition, and of possessing a vastly good Opinion of their own Deserts.

Notwithstanding this conception of his nature, however, the worthy Artist is a very modest Fellow, offering his Pictures to the Consideration of the World with not a little Trepidation to himself.

It is not often that one of the Limnor's Craft has such an Opportunity to present to his Patrons an Apology for his work, as the present Occasion offers to the Writer. It is with this advantage in his possession that he now undertakes to direct the Attention of the polite Reader to the Fact that the larger Part of the Pictures prefented to View in this Collection, is but a Portion of the Artift's Work which has been publifhed in Prints during the current Year. Thus he may boaft that, whatever the Offsprings of his Mufe may lack in Grace, fhe herfelf poffeffes a pretty great fecundity of productivenefs.

Moreover, the Artift may, perhaps, be allowed to claim for that Mufe that fhe is extremely American in her Inclinations, and for this Reafon he amufes himfelf with the Hope that the Publick may find fome Entertainment in thofe fimple and rural Scenes which he has endeavored to furround the characters he has depicted and of which his Patrons may, without doubt, have as perfect an Acquaintance as he himfelf may boaft of poffeffing.

The Reader, having thus been introduced to that Goddefs whom the Artift worfhips, may alfo, if he pleafes, obferve that this Catalogue (which was written for the better elucidation of the Work prefented) has been divided into Parts, fo that the Pictures fhall not be fcattered before his Attention in too aimlefs a Fafhion, but rather with fome Order as to their Purpofe.

PART FIRST—is intended to embrace a Collection of Drawings depicting certain Events occurring in the Life of GENERAL GEORGE WASHINGTON as well, alfo, of the Incidents bearing immediately upon his Career. Thefe Pictures were drawn to illuftrate a Series of very able and learned Thefes Bearing upon the Life of that Great Man written by Woodrow Wilfon, Efq.,

Profeffor

Profeſſor of Political Economy and Juriſprudence at Princeton Univerſity.

PART SECOND—contains a Series of Drawings illuſtrative of two Lucubrations of the Artiſt's own; the one preſented to a complacent Publick in Harper's New Monthly Magazine during the paſt Chriſtmas Seaſon, the other in Harper's Weekly Newſpaper of a like date—the one under Title "The Romance of an Ambrotype," the other being an Account of the appearance of the Ghoſt of Captain Brand, the Pirate.

PART THIRD—preſents to the kind Attention of the Publick, five Drawings (of a Set not yet complete) illuſtrating a very charming Story written by the ingenious Dr. S. Weir Mitchell and now running its courſe in the Century Magazine. In this Part is included a Drawing (as yet unpubliſhed)* illuſtrating a Paper upon Admiral Lord Nelſon, written by Captain Mahan.

PART FOURTH.—In this the Artiſt preſents a few of many Sketches made during a Journey upon a Canal Boat through the Northern and leſs populous Parts of the Commonwealth of New York.

PART FIFTH—preſents two sets of Pictures invented by the Artiſt to carry their own Story; the one done
ſeveral

---

*NOTE.—The Writer would here explain to his Patrons that the above appeared in the Firſt Edition of this Catalogue before the Century Magazine had publiſhed the Print in the current iſſue of that Periodical.

several Years ago entitled, "A Paſtoral Without Words;" the other produced at a later Period and entitled "By Land Sea."

PART SIXTH,—you may, if you pleaſe, conſider as a miſcellaneous group of Pictures done at various Times and upon ſeveral Occaſions.

This brief Preface is preſented to the candid Reader as a ſort of Apology for the Quantity of Pictures he is called upon to view. For, ſo arranged, they may ſeem to him to be of leſs Number and more ſimple in their Comprehenſibility than they otherwiſe would. Following this the Writer offers with ſome particularity, a detailed Catalogue of the various Works in their Order.

HOWARD PYLE.

TABLE.

In the Garden at Mount Vernon.

# A TABLE,

Of the feverall Parts mentioned in the Foregoing.

---

## PART FIRST.

A Set of feventeen full page Drawings Together with three leffer Paintings, defigned for Headbands and Tailpieces illuftrative of the Life of Gen. Wafhington.

---

No. 1.—HEADBAND For The Initial Paper.

This Picture prefents a fancied Likenefs of a Virginia Planter of a Time of about 1725. He is depicted as fmoking a Pipe of Tobacco—the Artift conceiving that to be typical of his Profeffion in Life. Behind him may be feen a Barque of the fame Period, ftudied with fome Particularity from Drawings and Prints of that Pattern of Veffel.

Upon

Upon the more diftant Shore you may fee, elevated upon the Cliff of Sand, a Group of Houfes, as of Yorktown.

No. 2. —A VIRGINIA Plantation Wharf.

This Scene is intended to reprefent a Barque (familiar to that depicted in No. 1,) taking on a Load of Tobacco at the Wharf of a Planter of confiderable Quality, who, himfelf, may be viewed feated upon Horfeback in Converfation with the Captain of the Veffel. At the fhed are Negro Slaves bufy rolling the Hogfheads of Tobacco aboard the Veffel.

No. 3.—"EVEN Sir William Berkeley, the Redoubtable Cavalier Governor, Saw That He Muft Yield."

This Picture reprefents Sir William Berkeley, figning the Capitulation of the Province of Virginia in the prefence of the three Parliamentary Commiffioners appointed to make that Demand upon him. The Artift can only boaft of one Portrait in this Group of Figures—that of William Clayborne, Efq., who ftands with his Fingers refting upon the Table and with his Back to the Window. Governor Berkeley may be known by his more pretentious Appearance. The Man in the buff Coat is Captain

Captain Curtis of the Guinea, Frigate; the other feated Figure is intended to reprefent Richard Bennet, Efq., who fucceeded Sir William in the Gubernatorial Chair.

No. 4.—"THEY Read Only Upon Occafions When The Weather Darkened."

It is the intention of the Artift in this Picture to reprefent the Life of a comfortable and well-circumftanced Planter of Virginia of the Period of 1740. From the particular Nicety with which he is dreffed, you are to fuppofe him waiting for fome Friends to come and join him at a Game of Cards. Meanwhile he is entertaining himfelf with reading fome fly and merry Tale while he awaits their Arrival.

No. 5.—WASHINGTON'S Retreat From Great Meadows.

In this Picture it is intended to reprefent the American Colonial Army as a confiderable Mob of Men, fome without Uniforms; wounded, bedragged, and wet with the chilling Rain which fell fo continually upon them during their miffortunate withdrawal from the Field of Military Operation againft the French at Great Meadows. Here you may fee no Formation into Ranks or Platoons, but only a wet and muddy crowd of men
tramping

tramping homeward with the young Chieftain, so glorious in after years, brooding with the utmost Depression of Spirits upon the initial Misfortune which he was destined afterward so splendidly to retrieve.

No. 6.—THE Burial of Braddock.

In this Picture it is to be observed that the Artist has made some attempt at Portraiture; that Officer standing immediately upon the left of the youthful Washington being intended to represent General, then Lieutenant Colonel Gage; he upon the left of Gage being intended to depict the Figure of General, then Captain Gates—both of whom were doubtless present upon that melancholy Occasion. It may also be observed that the Coffin was lowered into a Grave dug immediately in the middle of the Road over which the Cannons and Commissariat Wagons were presently driven so that all Signs of the Interment were forever obliterated. The youthful Washington himself, it may be remembered, read the burial Service over his dead Chief, and the deplorable Ceremony occurred early in the Morning before the Camp was yet fully astir.

No. 7.—WASHINGTON and Mary Phillipse.

It is to be confessed that the Artist has here

here taken a great deal of Liberty with the Portrait of Miſs Phillipſe, as generally known. Neverthelefs, it is to be hoped that ſuch is not unpermiſſable ſince the long, flowing Locks of the accepted Portrait are rather thoſe adopted for Afternoon or Evening than the Morning wear. The Cap beneath which the young Lady's Hair is here gathered is of a leſs ſtately ſort; for you may, if you pleaſe, conceive of the youthful Waſhington calling upon her in the Morning ſhortly before his Departure for Boſton, where he was received with ſo much polite Diſtinction.

**No. 8.—IN the Old Raleigh Tavern.**

We here ſee the Panorama of Drawings bringing us more cloſely to thoſe troubleous Times when the Rebellious Colonies were to tear themſelves looſe from the Boſom of the Mother Country. The Scene is intended to depict five of the great Patriot Leaders who are buſy diſcuſſing plans for the calling of a Colonial Congreſs. It repreſents one of the upper Rooms of the old Raleigh Tavern, which ſtood in Williamſburg, the then Capital City of Virginia.

It was indeed an Houſe moſt notable in its Aſſociations as meeting Place of thoſe great Men of the Day, nor can it be ſufficientl ciently regretted that it has been deftroyed. Says the famous Hiftorian, Loffing—"When "I vifited Williamfburg in December 1848 "the Front of the old Raleigh Tavern had "been torn down and a Building in modern "Style erected in its Place."

The new Houfe of which he fpeaks was intended for the gayer Purpofes of a Dancing Room.

From this the Artift's Patrons may fee why he has been obliged to depend upon his Imagination in depicting the little narrow Room into which opened the Light of a Dormer Window. It is only that fmall Group of great Men gathered there that he could venture to reprefent with any Precifion of Portraiture. He who ftands leaning over the Table is Thomas Jefferfon; the Face behind him is that of Richard Henry Lee; he who ftands with his Spectacles thruft upward upon his Head is the great Orator, Patrick Henry; he with the Pen in his Hand is F. L. Lee; he with his Back to the Spectator is Dabney Carr.

**No. 9.**—LEAVING Mount Vernon for the Congrefs of the Colonies.

Here again is fuch an attempt to render the various Likeneffes as the Artift has been able to achieve. In the Centre it is intended ed to reprefent the ftill youthful Wafhington. Upon his Left is Patrick Henry and upon his right is Edmund Pendleton. The three are reprefented as departing for the Congrefs or Convention of the Colonies to be held in Philadelphia. In the remoter Diftance you may fee the formal and pretentious Front of Mount Vernon, in Front of which (if you choofe to obferve fo narrowly) you may fee a minute Group of Figures ftill lingering upon the Lawn before the Doorway after the Adieus have been faid to thofe who were to take the long and arduous Journey to Philadelphia.

No. 10.—LADY Wafhington's Arrival at Headquarters, Cambridge.

The generous Reader is now, if he pleafes, to confider the pictorial Scene as having entered that more ftern and military Period of our great and good Hero's Life, when he had laid afide the Toga of the Statefman for the fterner Panoply of War. The beloved Confort of the great Man has juft arrived at Cambridge, and the Commander-in-Chief himfelf has haftened forth to meet her and to receive her into his Military Houfehold. Some of his Staff follow their Leader to add their Welcome, and

and a Group of curious Spectators ſtands obſerving the affecting Scene.

No. 11.—WASHINGTON and Steuben at Valley Forge.

In this the Artiſt preſents to his Patrons a View of that diſtinguiſhed Foreigner, the Baron Steuben, inſpecting, in the company of the Commander-in-Chief, the ſad Condition of the Patriot Army as it lies encamped upon the Hills about Valley Forge.

No. 12.—THE Eſcape of Arnold.

The Reader may here, if he pleaſes, ſee a Preſentment of the infamous Traitor, Benedict Arnold, as he appeared coming aboard the Engliſh Sloop-of-war, VULTURE, whither he had eſcaped from the deadly Indignation of his Chief after his nefarious Plot had been diſcovered.

The VULTURE having been fired upon by the Patriot Batteries from the Shore, it may be remembered, had dropped down to the Protection of the Highlands, where ſhe was at that Time lying anchored.

No. 13.—MUSTERED Out—A Reſt by the Wayſide.

You may here view the cloſe of that great Struggle for Independence, when the Patriot Army having been diſbanded, the Individuals

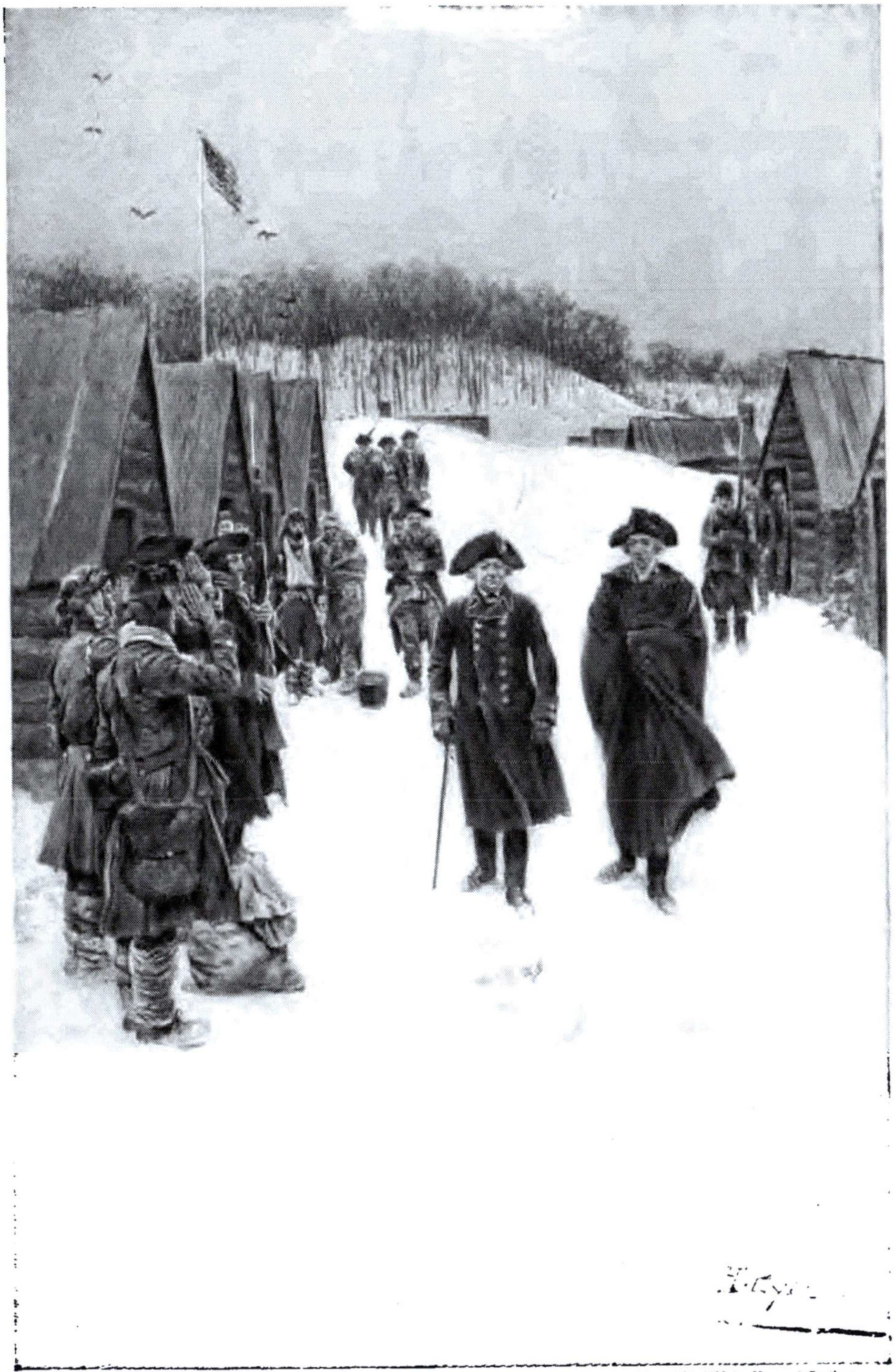

From Harper's Magazine.



At Valley Forge.

dividuals thereof found their way homeward as beſt they could, tattered, footſore and pennileſs. A Group of the weary Heroes is here repreſented as reſting in Front of a wayſide Tavern while Hard Cider is being ſerved out to them for their Refreſhment—the curious Loiterers ſtanding gazing at them the while.

No. 14.—WASHINGTON Bringing His Mother into the Ball Room, Frederickſburg.

You here ſee the great Chieftain, the late Leader of the Nation's Hoſt in armed War, conducting his aged Mother, with a filial Piety equal to his former Valor, into the gayety of the Ball Room at Frederickſburg. The people bow before him, delighting to do him Homage, not more for his paſt Deeds of Glory than for his preſent Virtues.

No. 15.—WASHINGTON In His Garden At Mount Vernon.

Here we behold the great Soldier dwelling, Cincinnatus-like, amid thoſe humble and bucolic Joys he held ſo dear, and to which he was ſo glad to return after the diſtracting Clamor of War. Of the Gardener to whom Waſhington is talking, the ingenious Profeſſor Wilſon ſays, "He a-
"greed

"greed with Philip Barter that if he would
"ferve him faithfully as gardener and keep
"fober at all other times, he would allow
"him four dollars at Chriftmas with which
"to be drunk four days and four nights, etc."

No. 16.—THE Clerk of Congrefs Announcing to Wafhington his election to the Prefidency.

Here the Hero is depicted receiving with that calm Referve that befitted him fo well, the Announcement of his Election to the Chief Magiftry of our Nation. The fealed Packet lies upon the Table, while Charles Thomfon, Efq., addreffes the great Man in Terms of refpectful Congratulation. The other Figures reprefent two Gentlemen of quality who accompanied Mr. Thomfon from Alexandria upon his grateful Miffion.

No. 17.—WASHINGTON and Nelly Cuftis.

We here fee, in the clofing Shadows of the great Man's Life, how he behaved in that clofer Circle of the Family. The Scene depicts the Eve of Mifs Eleanor Parke Cuftis' Marriage to Lawrence Lewis, Efq. The Hero clad, not in the grandeur of Royal State, but in the old War-worn Uniform of Commander-in-Chief of the Patriot Armies, preffes a chafte Salute upon the Brow of his beloved adopted Daughter.

No. 18.

No. 18.—THE Death of Waſhington.

Thus we come to that laſt ſad Scene where the grim Deſtroyer lays his irreligious Hand upon the Great and the Good as well as upon the Mean and the Vicious. The bereaved Wife ſitting at the Foot of the Bed, ſays calmly and collectedly, "Is he "gone?" The Figure kneeling beſide the Bed is intended for Tobias Lear, Eſq., the great Man's Private Secretary; the others preſent are Dr. Craik, who ſtands with his Hand to his Eyes and Dr. Brown who ſits gazing with fixed Grief upon the ſad Scene.

So does the Ending come to even the greateſt Endeavor and the higheſt Aſpiration.

---

Following are two minor Paintings for the illuſtration of Profeſſor Wilſon's Papers.

No. 19.—BRADDOCK'S Defeat. Battle of Monongahela.

This Picture repreſents the lamentable Defeat of General Braddock at the Battle of Monongahela, where, hemmed in by the Woods and diſtracted by the demoniacal yelling of unſeen and Savage Enemy, the Troops fell an eaſy Prey to the Storm of Deſtruction poured in upon them.

No. 20.

No. 20.—THE Capitol at Williamſburg.

As it appeared as the Houſe of Government of Virginia, and before it was deſtroyed by Fire in 1746.

---

Following are a few minor Drawings delineated with Pen and Ink.

No. 21.—IS a Fragment ſketched with Pen and Ink, repreſenting a Likeneſs of Lawrence Waſhington, Eſq., and a Picture of Mount Vernon in the Diſtance.

No. 22.—ALSO a Fragment drawn with Pen and Ink, repreſents General Waſhington as he appeared in Battle with the Troops preſſing forward to the Attack.

No. 23.—ALSO a Sketch with Pen and Ink repreſenting the illuſtrious Hero walking, in Converſation with the Marquis LaFayette, upon the Grounds in front of his Reſidence at Mount Vernon. Upon the ſame Sheet is a Sketch of General Waſhington's Sword embelliſhed with a Wreath of Laurel.

No. 24.—ALSO a Sketch with Pen and Ink, depicts Preſident Waſhington and his Cabinet. Oppoſite to the Chief Magiſtrate ſits Jefferſon, the Secretary of State; next to Jefferſon

Jefferſon is General Knox, Secretary of War; immediately behind his Chief ſits Alexander Hamilton, Eſq., Secretary of the Navy. Upon the ſame Sheet is a Sketch repreſenting Fame with burning Torch and olive Wreath. The Figure is draped in black as emblematic of Grief for the dead Hero.

## PART SECOND.

Illuſtration for two Stories Written by the Artiſt—the Ghoſt of Captain Brand, Publiſhed in Harper's Weekly Chriſtmas Number, and the Romance of an Ambrotype, Publiſhed in Harper's Magazine Alſo for Chriſtmas.

No. 25.—"CAPTAIN Malyoe Shot Captain Brand Through the Head."

In this effort of the Artiſt, is depicted the lamentable Murther of Captain Brand and his Gunner by two of their Aſſociates in Sin, within the Mouth of the Cobra River, as recounted in a Story entitled The Ghoſt of Captain Brand.

No. 26.

No. 26.—"SHE Would Sit Quite Still permitting Barnaby to Gaze at Her."

    In this the Hero and Heroine of the Story are reprefented as Lovers aboard a Pirate Veffel, they having been captured by thofe Freebooters as fully recounted in the Story above mentioned.

No. 27.—ARE a lot of Sketches with Pen and Ink intended to illuminate the Heading for each Chapter, as follows:

a. Headband drawn with Pen and Ink for Chapter I.
b. Headband drawn with Pen and Ink for Chapter II.
c. Headband drawn with Pen and Ink for Chapter III.
d. Headband drawn with Pen and Ink for Chapter IV.
e. Headband drawn with Pen and Ink for Chapter V.

---

As the following Lift of Pictures included in this Part is fufficiently explained by the Prints and the Text accompanying each Drawing, no further Remark is made upon them, other than to afford each a Title.

No. 28.—Illuminated Title for the Romance of an Ambrotype.

No. 29.—Curlett and his Ambrotype.

No. 30.—Young Men coming to Call.

No. 31.—The Recruiting Office.

                                      No. 32.

No. 32.—Father and Son.
No. 33.—At the Camp.
No. 34.—On the Edge of the Battle.
No. 35.—Malvern Hill.
No. 36.—In the Hofpital.
No. 37.—The Convalefcent.
No. 38.—Mifs Smith.
No. 39.—The Queftion.
No. 40.—Tailpiece.

## PART THIRD.

It is, perhaps, not neceffary for the Writer to particularize the firft five Drawings of this Part, for doubtlefs the intelligent Reader has already perufed the Story of HUGH WYNNE (now being printed in the Century Magazine for Dr. S. Weir Mitchell) with a clofe and continuous Intereft. Neverthelefs, he ventures upon a flight running Defcription to accompany each number.

No. 41.—"DIDST Thou Tell Them I Taught Thee?"

This reprefents Hugh Wynne, the Hero of the Story, as a little Child, returning from his firft Day at School, and received at the Houfe Door by his Mother, who awaits his coming.

No. 42.

No. 42.—"I will Teach Thee to Anſwer Thy Elder."

This depicts Hugh Wynne's Father threatening, in a Moment of Wrath, to chaſtiſe his Son for ſome fancied Affront the latter was thought to have put upon him. The Lady who reſtrains his angry Arm is our Hero's Aunt, Miſtreſs Gainor Wynne.

No. 43.—This repreſents Hugh Wynne ſtriking down his Couſin, who, in the public Preſence of drunken Carouſers in the Room of a Coffeehouſe, had offered an Affront to our Hero's Mother.

No. 44.—Hugh Wynne and Darthea Penniſton.

This repreſents the Hero and Heroine of the Story ſeated, each at a Diſh of Tea, upon the Lawn in front of Miſtreſs Gainor Wynne's Country Houſe.

No. 45. (As yet unpubliſhed.)

Here the Artiſt preſents to his Patrons a Portrait of Miſtreſs Gainor Wynne, mentioned above.

---

In addition to theſe Efforts, the Writer takes Pleaſure in offering to an intelligent Publick, the following Drawing (unpubliſhed at the preſent Writing)* which has been

*Note.—So printed in the Firſt Edition of this Catalogue.

been loaned for that Purpoſe by the Kindneſs of the Century Magazine.

No. 46.—Nelſon at the Battle of Copenhagen.

This Painting is intended to depict the great Naval Hero of England ſtanding upon the Poop Deck of his Flag-ſhip, ELEPHANT, quietly ſealing a Letter written for the Crown Prince of Denmark, whilſt about him rages the Din and Clamor of prodigious Battle. This Act he performed with the utmoſt calmneſs and collectedneſs of Demeanor. The Hero may be ſeen with his empty Sleeve pinned to the Boſom of his Coat. Next to him, holding the Letter whilſt he ſets his Seal upon the Wax, is Captain Foley, of the ELEPHANT. Behind the Hero waits Captain Theſiger, who was to carry the Miſſive to its Royal Deſtination. The Individual holding the lighted Candle is Mr. Thomas Wallis, the Purſer of the ELEPHANT.

The Poſition of the immediate Part of the Daniſh line of Battle is indicated by the Ships in the Diſtance. The Veſſel upon fire is the Flag-ſhip DONNESBORG, into which the ELEPHANT has juſt poured its final and fatal Broadſide of Cannon Shot. The Veſſel in the further Diſtance, ſtill firing into the

the ſtern Quarter of the ELEPHANT. is the Daniſh Veſſel KOINBORG.

The Artiſt owes his Thanks to Mr. Warren Sheppard for much of the Particularity of Detail repreſented in the Perſpective of the Poop Deck here depicted.

## PART FOURTH.

As the two Sets of pictures here tabulated need no Deſcription (the pictures of one Lot having the Text accompanying them, thoſe of the other requiring no Text to explain them) the ſeveral Drawings are ſimply entered in their Order as below obſerved.

The firſt Set of Pictures is entitled "By Land and Sea," and is as follows:

No. 47.—In The Woodcarver's Shop.

No. 48.—Text accompanying the above.

No. 49.—A Sailor's Sweetheart.

No. 50.—Text accompanying the above.

No. 51.—The Sailor's Wedding.

No. 52.—Text accompanying the above.

No. 53.—A Wreck From The Sea.

No. 54.—Text accompanying the above.

The

Copyright, 1897, by THE CENTURY CO.

The second Set of Pictures is entitled "A Paſtoral Without Words," and appears as follows:

No. 55.—A Picture conveying the Title.

No. 56.—Verſe I.

No. 57.—Verſe II.

No. 58.—Verſe III.

No. 59.—Verſe IV.

No. 60.—L'Envoy.

It may be ſaid for this latter ſet of Drawings (which was done in India Ink to imitate Miniature Painting) that they were produced ſeveral years ago, appearing in the Chriſtmas number of Scribner's Monthly, 1890.

## PART FIFTH.

In this is included ſome examples choſen from a number of Pictures intended to illuſtrate a Cruiſe upon a Canal Boat enjoyed by the Writer, and ſubſequently publiſhed in Harper's Magazine.

As they do not require eſpecial Deſcription, they are entered in their Order as below.

No. 61.—A Color Sketch of a Tow of Canal Boats, as ſeen in Perſpective Aſcending the Hudſon River.

No. 62.—THROUGH Inland Waters.
An Illuſtrated Title.

No. 63.

No. 63.—Building a Floating Town.

No. 64.—A Bumboat trading upon the Hudſon River.

No. 65.—On a Lumber Boat.

No. 66.—A Pair of Canuck Girls.

No. 67.—A Mother and Child.

No. 68.—In the Twilight.

No. 69.—A Sketch in Color of a Canal Lock in the Mountains of Northern New York.

No. 70.—The Canal Locks at Waterford.

No. 71.—A View on the Northern Canal.

No. 72.—A Mountaineer.

No. 73.—A Lock Keeper.

No. 74.—A Sketch on Lower Lake Champlain.

No. 75.—The Interior of the Boat.

No. 76.—A Tailpiece.

## PART SIXTH.

Miſcellaneous.

No. 77.—MORGAN at Porto Bello.

The Picture under this Title was drawn to illuſtrate a Poem by Edmund Clarence Stedman.

Stedman, Efq., which was publifhed in Harper's Magazine December 1888. It reprefents the great Buccaneer viewing certain of the Captives won by the Prowefs of his Arms againft the Spaniards.

It was kindly loaned for the prefent Exhibition by Mr. Stedman, the Owner.

No. 78.—EVENING in Old Manhattan.

This Drawing was done to illuftrate an hiftoric Sketch of New York, written by Thomas A. Janvier, Efq., and was publifhed in Harper's Magazine for the Month of May 1893. It depicts two Dutch Lovers of the Time enjoying their mutual Paffion befide the Banks of the Canal in old New York.

No. 79.—"PIRATES Sometimes Serve Their Captains fo.

The illuftration under this Title was made to decorate a Paper written by Thomas A. Janvier, Efq., and publifhed in Harper's Magazine of Nov. 1894.

The fcene depicts a Pirate Chieftain murthered by his Band. His Slayers may be feen departing in the Diftance leaving the Corpfe lying upon the Sand of that Defert Strand, while they depart to enjoy the Profits of their bloody Deed.

No. 80.

No. 80.—THE Surrender of Captain Pearfon.

This Drawing which was publifhed, together with a Paper upon John Paul Jones, which appeared in the Century Magazine for April 1895, illuftrates the Scene at the Clofe of the tremendous Engagement between the BONNE HOMME RICHARD under command of Captain John Paul Jones and the SERAPIS under command of Captain Pearfon. In it the Artift endeavors to reprefent the Manner in which Captain Pearfon came aboard the Veffel of his Conqueror and furrendered his Sword.

The Reader may, if he pleafes, obferve the Contraft between the neat and well-dreffed Appearance of the Britifh Commander; his Stockings only fpecked with Blood, and the difhevelled afpect of the American Victor. It was this Difference that won that famous Battle, for the one Captain ftood upon the Quarter Deck and ordered the Battle, and the other fought like a Demon with his Men.

No. 81.—"THE Admiral Came In His Gig of State."

This Drawing was made for a Poem written by J. J. Roche, Efq., and publifhed in the Century Magazine for June 1895. It depicts an Englifh Admiral petitioning a Dutch

Dutch Admiral, in the midſt of a Battle, to ſell him Powder enough to carry on the Engagement.

The great War Ship, upon the Deck of which the Dutch Admiral ſtands, was, in the conſtruction of this Picture, ſtudied with not a little nicety and with a great deal of Enjoyment by the Artiſt, from cotemporary Plates and Prints of Veſſels of its Sort.

No. 82.—THE Pirates' Chriſtmas.

This Picture was drawn for Harper's Weekly, Chriſtmas Number, of 1893. It repreſents the Situation of three Pirates who have been captured ſomewhere off the Coaſt of New England, and who are now enjoying their Chriſtmas in Chains with no very great Pleaſure to themſelves. The Gaoler has allowed them to exerciſe in the Gaol Yard, and is now ſhowing them, with a good deal of Satiſfaction, to a number of the Town's People, who, lead thither by Curioſity, have come to entertain themſelves with a View of the misfortunate Captives.

No. 83.—THE Werewolf.

This Depicts an Incident in a curious Story written by the late Eugene Field, Eſq., and publiſhed in the LADIES' HOME JOURNAL for March 1896.

No. 84.

No. 84.—LOVE at Valley Forge.

A Drawing made for the LADIES' HOME JOURNAL and publifhed for December 1896. It reprefents the Heroine of the Story petitioning the Commander-in-Chief to liberate her Lover, the Hero from captivity. The Scene depicts the Room of the Houfe which Wafhington ufed at Valley Forge.

With this the Artift brings the Lift of his Work to a clofe, trufting that whatever the Pictures prefented may lack in Merit, the Publick may grant that Approbation which, from its great generofity it hath always beftowed upon him.

THE END.

Printed by Libri Plureos GmbH in Hamburg, Germany